MetamorpHERsis

MetamorpHERsis

*Becoming The Woman You Desire
And All God Designed You to Be.*

TACONDRA L. BROWN

Copyright

Copyright © 2021 Tacondra L. Brown All Rights Reserved

MetamorpHERsis ™

Becoming The Woman You Desire and All That God Designed You to Be.

Printed in the United States of America.

No portion of this eBook may be reproduced or transmitted inany form or by any means except for brief quotations in printed reviews without the prior written permission of Tacondra L. Brown.

For information on bulk purchases, please contact:

info@tacondra.com

All scripture quotations are taken from New Living Translation, New King James Version, New International Versions, or the Amplified Bible.

All definitions obtained from Merriam-Webster.com

Interior Design: Tacondra L. Brown

Book Cover Design by C.M. Baker Design

ISBN: 978-0-9997802-1-3

DEDICATION

I dedicate this book to the beautiful butterfly who is intentional about healing from the pain of her past, embracing the beauty built within her, and morphing into the mature woman she desires, and all that God created her to be. Regardless of where you are in your process of becoming, remember that the best version of who you are was formed inside of you from the very beginning!
BE YOU!

Table of Contents

A LOVE LETTER TO HER 1

TRANSFORMATION GOD'S WAY 6

AWAKENED TO DESTINY 27

EAT TO GROW 43

THE POWER OF STRUGGLE 55

MADE TO SOAR 76

ABOUT THE AUTHOR 92

A LOVE LETTER TO HER

Hello Beautiful Butterfly! I am so excited that you invested in this book for your personal growth and development! If the topic of Becoming HER caught your attention, that means your next level is calling and God's unique expression of Himself in you in the earth is arising! Believe me when I say that we have not crossed paths by coincidence. It is by divine appointment that you have connected with me by reading this book. Our Heavenly Father knows exactly what you need and when you need it the most! Even when you do not think or know you need it! I share this from my own experience. You are more than likely reading this book because you are on a path to becoming the healed, empowered, and resilient woman God created, and it is my intention to help activate and inspire the transformative work in you so that even greater works can be done through you! I am excited to be on this journey with you. If this is your first time reading one of my books, I highly encourage you to learn more about me and my story of healing and transformation by reading my books: *Transformed from Pain to Purpose, Beautifully Transformed-Discovering Beauty in The Beast,* and *A 7-Day Healing and Transformation Devotional.* You can find these books on my website: www.tacondra.com or on amazon. I pour my heart into every page written, and I do it in a simple way for all to get an understanding. I pray that my gift of writing helps other women (and men) like me who have questions and are searching for answers, purpose, and significance. Are you a broken beauty? One who is scarred by past pains, hurt and trauma, and hiding behind masks of performance and perfection? Perhaps, you have felt broken, embarrassed, abandoned, sad, or timid in the past because of your life circumstances or conditions. Are you living a life controlled by fear and the opinions of people right now due to a need for affirmation, validation, and approval? Maybe a devastating loss or traumatic event you did not ask for in life crushed your courage, confidence, and belief in God, and yourself. It stripped you of an identity you once knew and left you with labels attached to your soul that do not define who you indeed are. Do you feel stuck and stagnant in your life? If you feel this way, I understand where you are. I know because I have felt the same way too. I have found that it does not matter what life has thrown at you, or what losses you have endured; it does not even matter what you have done to contribute to any pain, guilt, and shame in your life. The wisdom, words, and prayers penned in this book will remind you that God's best is not only ahead of you but also inside of you! No matter how ugly life can get, there is still beauty built within you that never fades. This beauty is constantly longing to come forth, arise, and shine bright! You, beloved, possess the power within to transform and BECOME all that you desire, and all God designed you to be for HIS glory! I am going to tell you all about this power within and how to make use of it! It is time for you to MetamorpHERsis!

TRANSFORMATION
GOD'S WAY

In the beginning, GOD… (Genesis 1:1). This is always a great place to start! Because God knew the end and the beginning before the beginning began. "He chose us in Him before the foundations of the world, that we should be holy and without blame before Him in love…" (Ephesians 1:4). You see, in the beginning was God, and the Word was with God, and the Word was God. In the beginning, with God, is where you and I were too; although, we were just a thought at that time. Indulge with me for a moment to ponder on this, will you? Not only were you on God's mind, heart, and a part of His master plan, but He fully knew you, loved you, and chose you before knitting you together in your mother's womb.

Not to forget, He looked at you, along with everything else that He made, and said, "it is very good!" (Genesis 1:31). If God said you were good, that settles it! You are mmm! mmm! Good! The real question is: Do you believe it? If not, I need you to get this truth anchored in your spirit!

The love God showed you and me from the start is the authentic portrait, example, and exact meaning of what I call beauty. Even His story of redemption through our Lord and Savior, Jesus Christ, is beautiful. Beauty is a gift that flows from God because He is beautiful, His Son is beautiful, and through Him, everything that was made was made beautifully! Without Him, Jesus Christ, nothing that was made has been made! (John 1:3) We were made by love and created to love Him and others! Of course, If you are familiar with our origin, Adam and Eve messed up in the garden of Eden. Their curiosity, appetite, and desire for significance outside of God led to their deception by the devil to become what they already were. Satan told them in Genesis 3:5, "...you will become like God..." when in fact, they were already created in God's image and likeness! I have quite a few questions for Adam and Eve when I get to heaven! It is not shameful to be deceived, but it is to stay deceived! They resorted to hiding from God due to shame and covering themselves in fig leaves. What embarrassing or distasteful acts have you committed that left you covered in fear, inadequacy, guilt, and shame? Those sins that cause you to run away from God and His grace rather than to Him! When God asked, "Adam, where are you?" He was not referring to their geographical location. God was talking about their spiritual position. Not only did Adam and Eve realize their naked condition because of the sin, but their spiritual position of being in the right fellowship with the Father also changed. If only Adam would have responded differently. I can only imagine how different our lives would be if Adam would have repented and allowed God to graciously reconcile them back to Him instead of shifting blame and searching for solutions to cover their sin. Like little toddlers, they resorted to hiding and denial after being caught red-handed yielding to acts and behaviors outside of Gods character. At times it is difficult to wrap our minds around the truth that God does not desire to cast us away when we sin (John 6:37). He is not a horrible Father waiting to throw down the harsh hammer of guilt and condemnation on us. Abba provided the ultimate solution to our sin, guilt, and shame. The answer is reconciliation to Him through Jesus Christ. Yet, we still find it conveniently inconvenient to try and find our own way. If it were not for Adam and Eve's imputed sin, we would not be afflicted with the consequences of our sinful nature and the fallen world we live in today. Just imagine how pleasant and peaceful life would be without death, inequality, injustice, hatred, war, laboring, sweat, pain, and tears! Unfortunately, that is not the kind of world we live in today. But thanks be to God for His Son Jesus and the finished work He accomplished on the cross. He became a slave to sin on the cross so that we could become Sons of God. He became broken so that you and I could be made whole. Jesus became like you and me in the flesh; He was born under the law, to redeem us, so that we might obtain full rights to become like Him. You are saved from your past life by Him. Your future is found in and through Him, and your transformation is indeed all about HIM! Jesus Christ is the foundation! He is the base, the boundary, the balance, and the beauty of what your life is all about!

Without knowing your position of authority, the power of His Holy Spirit within you, and your purpose in HIM, you will always search for your significance outside of whom God created you to be. Knowing this fundamental.

Now, let us have a conversation as to what MetamorpHERsis is all about! I know. The word may be somewhat difficult to pronounce. But if you say it slowly, you will get the gist of it! *META-MORP-HER-SIS!* Did you catch it? If this word is not ringing in your spirit or making sense, do not worry. By the time you finish reading this book, I am certain it will be clear and have more meaning to you. So, tell me. What comes to mind when you say this word? Is it caterpillars? Growth? Struggles? Butterflies? Well, you are right about all of that. In its simplest form, metamorpHERsis is all about transformation. Not just any transformation but transformation God's way! He is the Designer, Creator, and Initiator of it all! His way of transformation is done with little self-effort.

His process of transformation requires you to know and believe the truth about who He created you to be at your core! Your spirit! The world teaches us that change happens on the outside and then the inside. But the truth is that significant change must always occur on the inside first. It is a change that originates from your soul and spirit, and not from your ego or who others expect you to be. MetamorpHERsis is about becoming healed, empowered, resilient, and relinquishing the old version of you to become the best version of you!

The woman God designed when He formed you inside of your mother's womb. Transformation is a radical act or process of change in the mind, body, and soul. It involves a conversion in your form, thinking, appearance, and actions. Here is a key pearl about true transformation that most do not realize: Whenever you find something about yourself you do not like and want to change, you need to pray and ask God for the grace to reinvent it. Throughout my own journey, I have discovered that there are two primary ways we transform:

1. From the inside out.

2. By seeing yourself outside of yourself, and *beyond* your current state or condition.

INSIDE OUT

Transformation is an internal process with an external result. This is one of the reasons why healing the inner you is fundamental to becoming the best you! Thinking that an appealing outward appearance will correct your internal inadequacies is only a temporary fix. Beauty is fleeting (*see Proverbs 31:30*). Many are falling for the trap of having pretense but lacking power and substance on the inside. We are likely to yield to this pattern when searching for importance and meaning in life. I have learned the hard way that temporary solutions are just that; momentary. When changing your exterior becomes the focus and you neglect to heal, develop, and nurture your soul, mind, heart, and emotions, it ultimately leaves you empty and frustrated. It delays the real manifestation of who you indeed are. This manifestation I am referring to is the Heavenly Father's image of you.

God is your Creator, and He designed you in His image and likeness. You were created to display His glory, not your own. Transformation is not accomplished through your own self-effort. It is solely a work of God and the power of His Holy Spirit within you.

This transformative work is not always seen at once. But even when you do not feel it or see it, trust that transformation God's way is happening.

Real transformation begins by taking a good look at yourself in the mirror. In fact, that is always a great place to start when you desire to change something about yourself. Michael Jackson taught us that. But do not stop there. You might get overwhelmed or even feel depressed by the work to be done. Not knowing how or where to start is half the battle! In fact, this is one of the main reasons why most people get stuck and remain comfortable staying the same. Change is hard! It is even more tough trying to change when you do not know what to pray and ask God for, when you are not afforded the pleasure of having an example to model after, and you are the trailblazer in your family.

The best advice is to start with the truth. Tell God about your struggles. Cast all your cares, worries, and desires onto Him. He really does care about the things you do, and He is waiting for you to invite Him into those hard, stubborn spaces in your life so He can transform them. You must see yourself as a work of art, always in progress. You are always growing, stretching, and asking God for the grace to see yourself the way He sees you.

SEEING YOURSELF OUTSIDE OF YOURSELF

"Meta" is a word or prefix meaning: *"beyond"* or *"transcending"*. Do not allow your current circumstances and conditions to define you. Allow God to help you reinvent things about yourself that you do not like. And be ready to receive the hard truths when the Holy Spirit shines a light on the dark areas of your heart. God will even send people across your path to show you what is in you! Good and bad! This process of seeing yourself outside of yourself is not always a walk on the beach. You will discover things you love about yourself and things you do not like at all. You may even be in denial about the vile issues hidden in your heart. Pride, arrogance, selfishness, anger, competition, and foulness, amongst many other issues, to name a few. Do not allow your flaws and imperfections to discourage you though. The real power is in confronting the inner you that is blocking you from embracing your authentic self on the path of discovering all God designed you to be. You may even wonder at times, "why is it so hard for me to become the woman I desire?" Well, you may be one of those reasons. That is a hard pill to swallow, but you may not realize that you are your own stumbling block.

Do not worry, though; you are not a lost cause or a horrible person. And you are not the only one holding yourself back. Trust me. There are plenty of others like you and me who battle with the same things daily. Some other reasons you may be experiencing a delay in your becoming is due to fear of the unknown, not knowing how to change, and even the company you keep can hold you back. Do yourself a favor and get in the right environment. There is not just transformation in the right community but powerful healing as well.

I want to talk about the real reason why you are reading this book. More than likely, you are a woman who has been wounded. Something is blocking the transformation you desire. Perhaps, you have suffered trauma or experienced a loss in life that has left you paralyzed with fear, shame, guilt, doubt, and unbelief. Whether it is a job loss, divorce, the death of a loved one, or even a physical loss in your body, you lost something that once determined your worth, defined who you were, or gave your life meaning, and it has left you stuck in a place you cannot seem to get out of. When you evaluate your life right now, you may feel inadequate, not good enough, and unable to produce or give birth to new ideas. Or you give up easily! Are you tired of living below your potential and being confused about your purpose? I will even add that you are frustrated and overly critical of yourself, and you self-sabotage by causing problems or blockages in your life that restrict your growth and positive development.

Deep down inside, you want to change, but you do not know how or what is holding you back. Fear of the unknown terrifies you. Am I all up in your life right about now? If not, then you may be reading the right book but at the wrong time. But you *are* reading the right book at the right time if you can relate to these struggles. I know how you feel because I was once like you too! I have felt the same feelings and emotions before.

To be honest, I still experience them at times. But knowing the truth sets you free from being ruled by feelings and emotions. I have worn the masks of confidence and contentment on the outside while feeling broken and empty inside. I recognize the weight of carrying unresolved pain, and I am well-acquainted with fear, unbelief, and the negative voices in your head that shout, "you're not good enough for your own pity!" You cannot go back and change the past, but you can move forward, believing that whatever transpired did not happen to you but for you! It happened to become stronger, wiser, more flexible, aware, and understanding of life challenges. You see, God does not orchestrate the bad in our lives; however, he can cause all things to work together for good for those who love Him and are called according to His purpose (Romans 8:28). He is the master of turning negatives into positives! Here is where I have the privilege of giving you hope.

Everything you need to become HER and experience resiliency in your life is already inside of you. You must BE before you BECOME HER! I know, you might not believe you possess the gifts, talents, treasures, and superpowers necessary to fulfill your destiny. But you do! For some reason, it is often easy for us to trust and invest in what everyone else is carrying rather than ourselves. Beloved, what you carry is enough, and everything inside of you is worthy and extremely valuable. That is why your transformation from the inside out is necessary! What is inside of you must come forth! All that you are and all that you will be is embodied within you and your struggle of becoming.

In the same way that the struggle is essential to the caterpillar's process of becoming a butterfly! You have the power to become HER when you stop looking outside of yourself to find HER. Again, everything you need to live on purpose and with a purpose is already inside of you. Look at the words Introspection, Intuition, and Instincts. God placed His knowledge and the unique expression of Himself on the inside of you! The blessings of God rest in what He created you to be, not what you create (*see Genesis 1:26-28*). This means you do not need to act, be, live, look, or talk like someone else to be blessed better. BE YOU! Trying to become anything outside of what God created you to be places you outside of His grace and your gifting. It is exhausting trying to be someone you are not! You are different by design and uniquely graced to be you and do you! And you better believe that nobody else can do you like you do!

Unfortunately, devastating losses, trauma, and tragedies in life often have a way of robbing you of your identity; causing you to forget who you are and leaving you feeling inadequate, lost, confused, stuck, and unable to soar in life. This book was written to help heal, empower, and inspire your transformation into the resilient, beautiful woman you are! While this book does not contain all that I desire to impart to you, it will provide you with a glimpse of what mentoring with me consists of. I will guide you through a 4-step process of Becoming HER. The wisdom, insight, and instructions written will help you gain clarity to identify where you are in your transformative process. Do not forget your Becoming HER transformation journal also to answer the questions asked, take note of the precious pearls dropped throughout the pages, to journal your thoughts, and whatever the Holy Spirit reveals to you during this time. I hope you are ready to dive deeper into this! Let's go!

AWAKENED TO DESTINY

AWAKENING
STAGE 1: EGG

"for the light makes everything visible. This is why it is said, "Awake, O sleeper, rise up from the dead, and Christ will give you light." Ephesians 5:14

*I*f you are asleep, now is the time to WAKE UP! This is the first stage of transformation. I call it the "awakening" stage. You are awakening out of a form familiar to you and everyone else, into a heightened state of awareness and newness. This might seem scary initially because it involves becoming aware that something is not right, off, or different about you. Your eyes are opened to see through the lies and illusions that hurt, pain, and past trauma have created. You may feel unfulfilled and frustrated with the progress or lack thereof you have made in your life. Something deep inside of you desires more. You want to do more. Become better. You desire for your life, career, pursuits, and relationships to be more fulfilling, richer, and whole. You are tired of experiencing the same negative thoughts, emotions, and disappointments in life that you have settled with as your reality.

You may even battle with aches and pains in your body that will not go away. If you can relate to any of this, I imagine you screaming inside your head, "enough is enough!" Honey, your soul is crying for freedom! What is happening is the realization that you have been living life with unresolved pain and hurts from the past, and that your heart needs healing. The issues you do not allow God to deal with in you will rule over you. That is not The Father's desire for you! His desire is for you to rule and reign over every circumstance on the earth!

The "H" in "HER" is for **HEALED**! There is no point in becoming a better you if you are not going to be intentional about letting God heal the hurt and broken places inside you. God wants to heal your hurt, your heart, and unhealthy habits that were formed because of your trauma. I ran away from my healing for years because it meant that I would have to change! It meant that I would have to let go of my pain and all the false benefits that came with it. The sense of entitlement, anger, unforgiveness, resentment, my comfort, amongst other things I indulged in to numb my pain. I did not want to let go of my normal dysfunction, nor did I desire to experience a different type of hurt. There is more healing than there are hurts when you surrender to God's process of restoration. It takes pain to get rid of pain, therefore, you must choose your hurt. Either you will choose to remain the same and stay stuck wallowing in old pain, or you will embrace the new pain of becoming better. My desire for you is to make healing and wholeness something you move towards rather than continuously running away from. When you avoid healing you subconsciously choose to sit in hurt, unforgiveness, and bitterness, amongst many other negative emotions. There is something better on the other side of bitterness. There is restoration on the other side of resentment. Your freedom is felt, and faith is increased when you choose to forgive.

Notice, the keyword here is: choose! Forgiveness is not attached to how you feel; it is a choice that empowers you and not those who have offended you. Unforgiveness can cause you to feel dry, stuck, and in bondage to people without even realizing there is a debt in your soul. A fresh rain of God's spirit is unable to flow freely through you because unforgiveness blocks the process of healing and the power of God in your life. What is the fruit of unforgiveness costing you in your life? Is it your health? Problems in your finances? Poverty and lack? Unforgiveness is too expensive! And there is no hurt, pain, or offense worth paying the price of living your life imprisoned. Ask the Holy Spirit to reveal the areas in your heart in need of healing that are attached to unforgiveness. Ask God for forgiveness, and forgive yourself for the hurt you have caused yourself and others. Forgive your offenders for causing you pain and start forgiving now. You are responsible for your own response to God. If God can forgive you for your sins repeatedly, then you too have the power to forgive others. You also can forget the offenses. We often say, "I can forgive but I cannot forget." This statement alone will keep you entrapped. You are not protecting yourself from future hurts by refusing to forget. In fact, you only open the door for the enemy to torment you even more by not allowing God to heal the hurtful memories of your past. The truth is that we have access to God's sea of forgetfulness. The question is: Will you make use of it? Remember, if God can forget, so can we! Free yourself from the debts, dejections, and detriments of unforgiveness.

Have you ever walked through what is called a dark night of the soul? If you are unsure of what that is, allow me to help you. If you have ever felt completely lost, hopeless, consumed with depression and unimaginable pain, then you have experienced this phenomenon. As I reflect on my own journey, I can say that my nights of the soul helped build who I am today. Those moments taught me so much about my life purpose now, even though I experienced unimaginable pain and inner turmoil. One of my favorite scriptures in the 23rd Psalms says, "Though I walk through the valley of the shadow of death I will fear no evil, for thou art with me."

I want you to understand that what you are really walking through is a shadow when dark seasons arise. Shadows are formed when an object, in this case, the lies of the enemy, the dark life circumstances, events, and trauma meant to break you, are blocking you from seeing the light. The truth is the light! Hence, the reason all you can see is a shadow in the darkness! What is going on around you is an illusion meant to blind you from the truth that God loves you; He will never leave you or forsake you, and He is hurt by the things that hurt you. This scripture encourages and gives you hope knowing that you do not have to go through valley seasons alone, feeling fearful or abandoned.

Persevere through the valley and get to the other side. Our Heavenly Father is with you! There is not only light at the end of the tunnel, but you are the light inside the tunnel. You carry God's love, light, and Holy Spirit within you! The last thing you want is to get stuck in a dark, sunken place the way I did. Most people do not learn how to cope with the effects of trauma successfully and cannot move forward from painful life events.

This results in getting stuck in a cycle of experiencing post-traumatic stress disorder and you are left with negative emotions, unwanted memories, broken beliefs, and triggers from what you experienced or witnessed. Healing your heart consists of dealing with matters of the mind, emotions, and soul. Healing from the sting of hurt or physical wounds can seem easier than healing your emotions because emotional healing requires work. It involves digging deep into the experiences and emotions that control you and taking your power back. This is essential because if you do not repair your emotions, you will repeat harmful and negative behaviors and patterns that sabotage your growth. Just because your wounds are not visible does not mean they do not exist. Mental and psychological wounds can be more damaging than physical wounds, and if left untreated, can lead to other serious mental and health-related problems. We have been taught that time heals all wounds, and that is not the truth. Time itself does not heal all wounds. If that were the case, you would be far better off than you currently are in your healing journey, right? There are layers to healing that require work! The process you go through spiritually, mentally, emotionally, and physically, and time is what heals wounds. Do not forget that wounds become scars too. After an injury or surgery, the body automatically works to repair wounds. As the skin heals, scars may form. This is a natural part of the process.

There are different types of scars: physical, emotional, mental, and spiritual scars. You may have a combination of these scars—physical scars from trauma, abuse, assault, or a physical loss to your body. Emotional and mental scars are inward because of verbal, mental, or emotional abuse. Spiritual hurts are deeply rooted inside of your soul and usually are not visible until later in life. They are the most damaging because they may or may not affect you, but they will certainly affect those around you. Doctors usually prescribe topical ointments for you to apply to physical wounds to help minimize scarring.

The Lord wants you to uncover the scars from hurt, pain, and losses you have endured in His presence so that He can heal them. He wants to prescribe His healing balm for your wounds and scars. This "balm in Gilead" to make the wounded whole is called the Holy Spirit. (*Reference Jeremiah 46:11*). Are you covering your scars instead of revealing them to the Father? God cannot heal what you are hiding. Wounds left covered or even uncovered for too long will not heal properly. As humans, we have a natural tendency to hide scars that are ugly and remind us of our pain. But God cannot heal what you are hiding. Granted, yes, He is all-knowing, but He is not intrusive. He will not force you to expose anything about yourself against your own will. He only invites you to open your heart to the truth. Your Heavenly Father loves you too much to leave you the way you are. But the question is, do you love yourself enough to want to change? Are you willing to surrender your way for His will? His process? Scars are meant to remind you that you are healed. The visibility of the scars depends on how you care for them. If you treat your scars like they do not exist, they are not going to disappear. This "inner awakening" stage is not something you should fear. This phase is associated with unusual feelings and emotions that often bring new benefits of post-traumatic growth. Embrace this feeling because it marks the beginning of your inner-healing journey.

Questions to Help Identify If You Are in This Stage:

1. What traumatic event occurred in your life? Something abrupt and unplanned that has changed your normal way of living, thinking, being, and doing?

2. What are you tired of in your life? What do you want more of?

3. Reflect on your life to understand how you have gotten to your present. What do you notice?

Explore these questions by digging deeper and expressing what you are feeling. This is necessary for your growth!

A PRAYER TO HEAL HER

Father, I humbly come to you to talk about the hurts, pains, spiritual and emotional wounds and scars my heart has suffered. I ask for your forgiveness as I forgive those who have offended me. I call upon you to heal me, Oh Lord, and I will be healed by your power! Save me and I will be saved! (Jeremiah 17:14) I trust and believe that you heal and are close to the brokenhearted, only you can bind up my wounds, and save me from being crushed in spirit. I surrender the keys to my heart to you, Lord. Give me a new heart and put a new spirit within me. Remove the heart of stone and give me a heart of flesh! (Ezekiel 36:26) I give you praise for wiping every tear from my eye, for rescuing me, and for saving me from my distress! In Jesus' name, Amen!

EAT TO GROW

STAGE 2: GROWTH CATERPILLAR (LARVA)

Growth: "The process of increasing in physical size"

I did not always appreciate my worth as a caterpillar because I was deceived into thinking that I had no purpose or value. I did not like the body I was in, most of the time I felt I was living life aimlessly and without purpose, I even wanted to be someone else because being myself was too much! Or not enough, really. Are these things you struggle with? If so, you are not alone. I believe we all battle with issues like this at some point or another. When we look at a caterpillar in the natural, sadly, most people diminish its worth until the glory of transforming into a butterfly is visible. We magnify the place of struggle (chrysalis stage), where the butterfly gains its wings, but we rarely recognize the first challenge the caterpillar deals with. Growing! It must stretch, grow, and shed old skin for the new skin required to metamorphose. The best type of pain you will ever experience is growing pains. But it is indeed a process that requires endurance. This is where the "E" in HER comes into motion. **Be EMPOWERED** to grow! You have permission to gain the knowledge, confidence, skills, and abilities necessary for your next! Growing involves changing your actions, making different choices, deciding to trust what God has placed inside you, and showing more care and compassion for yourself!

Growing might be difficult and hard to understand if you

are not used to being stretched beyond your comfort. But during this stage, there is a deep hunger for more. You may start by discovering the deep wounds, illusions, broken beliefs, and patterns that hinder you and then seek truths and explanations that will nourish and benefit your growth spiritually, mentally, emotionally, and physically. In this stage, you are seeking answers and asking allthe deep questions. You are in search of your life purpose, destiny, and the meaning of all that has happened in your life upuntil this point! Your perception of the reality around you changes. You may have a heightened sensitivity and feel disturbed by some of the things you will see and hear now than you did in your previous state of numbness or unawareness.

Be careful in this state as you are more likely to seek new

teachers, spirituality, and doctrines that can potentially answer your deep questions and try to fill the voids in your heart. The last things you want to attract are counterfeits and familiar spirits posing as the authentic teachers, mentors, the Holy Spirit, and substance worthy of filling your empty cup. The saying is: when the student is ready, the teacher will come. This is indeed the truth. Usually, the false teachers will always show up first; they are often the loudest and quickly come through the front door. That is not the way God works. Abba always comes through the back door, He operates slowly and with grace, and His voice is still and small. In this stage, you must also come to terms with truths about yourself you will not like. Do not utilize prayer and over-spiritualization as a defense mechanism or "scapegoat" to not ward off the enemies of your soul in this stage.

What I meanby that is, face the demons of your existence! Take a long, hard look in the mirror and face the INNER-ME. You will discover the enemies of your soul you have overlooked for years. The demons of fear, anxiety, low self-esteem, self-worth, laziness, procrastination, and self-sabotaging behaviors to name a few. Those "demons" have become your greatest hindrance to developing courage, authenticity, wholeness, and your full potential. Sit down and be honest with yourself about where you are and where you are going.

Identifying and outgrowing old ways, habits, mindsets, and even people can be frustrating, but it is part of the process. Be mindful of your circle in this stage. It would help if you surrounded yourself with like-minded individuals who have been or are currently traversing a straight and similar path as yours. These people will add value to your process; they will come with peace, patience, power, and understanding to propel you toward your destiny. They will feed your faith, sharpen you, encourage your growth, cry with you, and nurture your heart along the journey. Some of these people will also serve as catalysts for healing the deeply rooted hurts within your soul and spirit. There is healing and freedom in the right fellowship! It would be wise to use their journey as a mirror to reflect, compare, and contrast the details, strengths, and struggles of your journey. Most importantly, remember that it takes patience to grow! I will say that again. **IT TAKES PATIENCE TO GROW!**

So, give yourself the grace to grow during your process. You will read more about this in the next stage.

Eight Pearls to Empower HER Growth:

1. **Focus on activating your authenticity**: Discover who you are at your core and rest in whom God designed you to be. What do you like or dislike? What are you passionate about? What makes you different from everyone else? Focus on your strengths and develop them!

2. **Keep your eyes on your lane and not others:** God gives you the grace to run your race, not theirs.

3. **Open your heart to receive all that God has for you:** Exploring new opportunities to grow and opening your heart to others can be scary. Do it anyway. You

may not discern the heart and motives of people all the time, but rest knowing that your Heavenly Father does.

4. **Trust Yourself:** Do not allow the mistakes of your past to keep you from trusting the decisions you must make for your future.

5. **Invest in yourself:** You are your greatest investment! You can always expect a return from banking on yourself! Take a new class, hire a coach, find a mentor, learn a new skill or hobby! Buy a business! Do something different! Challenge yourself and do not be afraid to spend money on your growth! If something seems expensive, I challenge you to view it as being expansive! Do not fear investing in yourself at the level in which you want every area of your life to live

and thrive in.

6. **Make self-love and care a priority:** You love others AS MUCH AS you love yourself. This does not mean you cannot love others until you love yourself first. It is okay to do both at the same time!

7. **Give yourself grace:** Remember that you are not perfect. Embrace your flaws and imperfect perfections.

8. **Connect with Community:** Your network is your NETWORTH! If you want to increase in value, expand your community! God places His wealthiest resources in people.

Questions to Identify If You Are in A Growing Stage:

1. Do you sense an increased desire to know more about your true self as a person and how you can live a purposeful and balanced life?

2. Do you feel pressure to prepare for change in your life, although you are not quite sure exactly what that looks like?

3. In what ways do you feel your capacity or understanding is being stretched in this season of your life? *(for example, are you desiring to learn new things or do things you have never done before.)*

What you do in this stage is crucial to sustaining you through the next stage.

A PRAYER TO EMPOWER HER

Heavenly Father, I thank you for your Holy Spirit who empowers me not to lose heart in moments where I feel discouraged, defeated, and derailed by disappointments. Empower my thoughts, my actions, my growth, my voice, and my belief! Cause my mind to be renewed and transformed! I cast down every ungodly belief, every vain imagination, and I take captive every thought that would try to exalt itself above the word of God concerning the truth about me. I am what the Word of God says I am! Give me a deeper understanding of your Word and your ways! Fill me with your power, surround me with your presence, and soak me in your significance as I go deeper with you. I thank you that no weapon formed against me shall prosper! I come against every attack of the enemy to stagnate and stunt my growth to prevent me from going higher in you! I render them void, useless, and powerless in the name of Jesus! Every part of my being blesses the Lord! In Jesus' name, Amen!

THE POWER OF STRUGGLE

STAGE 3: METAMORPHERSIS COCOON (CHRYSALIS)

*I*n my first book, I promised that I would never harm a chubby caterpillar again. At least not intentionally, anyway. One day I was sitting outside on the back porch and this fuzzy caterpillar came crawling from out the grass, onto the porch, and towards the brick wall near me. I then watched as the caterpillar began to slowly make its way up the brick wall. I watched in awe for a moment and figured it did not know where it was going. So, I tried to help the caterpillar by placing it back into the grass, hoping it would eat more and head in a different direction.

Three times I watched this caterpillar crawl back from the grass, across the porch, and back up the brick wall. "I see that you are a little resilient caterpillar!" I whispered. My daughter eventually came outside to admire the fuzzy caterpillar with me. "Can we keep it?" she exclaimed. She loves listening to music, so she placed her headphones near the caterpillar's head and danced with it. I had her watch as I put the caterpillar back in the grass! Sure enough, the caterpillar moved quickly and with precision from the green grass, across the porch, and back to the brick wall, it began to crawl up.

Was the caterpillar searching for something? If so, what? What could it possibly be looking for up a brick wall? There is a story and a lesson to be learned in everything if we open our ears to hear and eyes to see. I asked the Lord, "What are you saying and showing me?" It did not dawn on me until later that evening what God was revealing. You see, the caterpillar was ready to transform. It was looking for a place to form its cocoon/chrysalis. This resilient caterpillar wandered away from the grass because it no longer needed to eat and grow. It was ready to go higher! Although I had good intentions, I kept placing the caterpillar back in an environment that no longer suited its growth. The caterpillar reached its capacity to grow in its current state and was ready for its next level, the place of struggle.

Looking from the outside, you may appear to be good and resting in your cocoon, but inside is where the struggle is taking place. This stage is the most painful yet pressing period. Its process involves struggle that often goes unnoticed. Everything about you on the inside changes while everything else on the outside looks and feels the same. Although you do not see it, you are relinquishing one form for another. Remember, earlier I mentioned it takes patience to grow! It takes patience to mature through your transformative process, just like the maturation or "metamorphosis" of a butterfly. The cocoon stage requires a level of letting go that you will endure slowly. This struggle is essential to your process of becoming all God designed, just like a caterpillar's struggle is essential to becoming a butterfly.

You are Empowered to become unchained from what is hindering your healing and freedom! The "**R**" in HER is fundamental in this stage and the next. You must be **RESILIENT** to overcome every obstacle you face. Part of this process within the cocoon phase still involves coming face-to-face with your past and pain. You must acknowledge what happened to you and understand that although you may not have been responsible for the loss you suffered, you are powerless to go back and change the past. You cannot go back and create a new beginning, but you can start again and create a new ending. Allow yourself to feel and process the emotions of the hurt, anger, frustration, grief, shame, and more. What happened to you is real. It is okay to stand in the facts of your realities, the key is not getting stuck there.

Restoration is also taking place during this phase. Restoration is the action of returning something to a former owner, place, or condition. Romans 12:2 says, "Be not conformed to this world but be transformed by the renewing of your mind." The first words of this sentence, "BE NOT conformed," insinuates that we were not made to BE like the world. To see as the world sees, do, act, or conform to the world's patterns. This sinful world's ways and views are not God's original design or pattern. Therefore, a transformation and renewing of the mind must happen to restore you to God's original design for you and His perspective of you! Part of your healing involves identifying deeply rooted lie-based beliefs in your heart that prevent you from becoming the person you desire, and all God designed.

Knowledge comes from information, and your worldview is shaped by the information you receive and your experiences. When you have had traumatic experiences, your mind will create stories and beliefs that are not true about yourself, others, and God. I call these broken beliefs. These beliefs are far from God's truth about you, others, and who He is. It only takes one hurt to form the perfect lie. And the perfect lie is the one that appears to be true based on the facts of your experiences.

I had an emergency hysterectomy at the age of 18 that left me barren after giving birth to my one and only daughter. As a result of this experience, I lived most of my life feeling barren, empty, unfruitful, and unproductive. I gave up on anything I started and aborted any new ideas because I believed I did not have the capacity to carry it full term and give birth. Believing God for anything for myself became nonexistent because I could not believe in God's love for me because of the lies my trauma told me. The feelings of anger and disappointment with God made it impossible for me to believe or even expect anything good from God. After all, how can you expect anything good from a God you are offended with, right? I experienced mental torment most of my life from fear, broken beliefs, and the lies I believed that the enemy said about me.

The lie that I was unworthy, inadequate, broken, barren, damaged and more resulted in me rejecting myself and telling myself even more lies. I masked my misery by becoming a performer to please people to feel worthy and accepted. I hid behind perfection and held myself to standards I would not even hold others to. I would not be telling the truth if I said that I do not still have my days of struggle. I am fully aware of my imperfections! Are you? One thing is for certain, I thank God for grace and the renewing of my mind, daily. The difference now is that I know the truth about me and God's love for me. I came to the realization that perfection is the perfect deception! I discovered that a barren womb in the natural cannot stop me from bearing, carrying, and giving birth to all that God has blessed me to give life to in the spirit! The truth is what sets you free! Truth is not only a principle: "a fundamental truth or proposition that serves as a foundation for a belief system, behavior, or for a chain of reasoning." Truth is a person! That person being Jesus Christ!

> "I am the way the truth and the life. No one comes to the Father except through me." John 14:6 (NIV)

If truth is a person, then that also means that truth has a nature, a character, and is **LIFE-GIVING**! That means there is freedom in it! Scripture says in John 8:32, "Then you will know the truth, and the truth will set you free." You cannot live out the truth by believing a lie! And the most dangerous lies are often the ones you tell yourself! Yes, the defense mechanisms and wounded thought patterns you have developed to protect yourself from future hurt and pain are lies! They may be protecting you from people, but they are also protecting you from the real you. If your belief paradigm is broken, you will not grow or reach your full potential. There must be a shift in your perspective of how you view yourself, others, and God! Part of healing and becoming empowered is identifying the deeply rooted lie-based beliefs in your heart. Satan is the Father of lies, it is his native language, and there is no truth in him, according to John 8:44. I came to the realization that a good father never lies to his children. He will always speak the truth in love, to build, encourage, and affirm his acceptance of you, even when the truth hurts. Is it easier for you to believe a lie than the truth? If so, my question to you is: Who is your father? Are you a child of God or Satan? I hope you are certain that you are a child of God!

Every lie of the enemy must be uprooted, every vain imagination, every ungodly belief must be cast down and replaced with the truth! If you are not certain how to do that, I have provided a formula for you to implement that will help identify, uproot, and replace broken beliefs. This formula requires you to do some deep soul searching and work! Do not skip through this because you wish to avoid reliving certain emotions, experiences in the past, or having an honest conversation with yourself.

It would be best for you to stop reading at this point if you are not ready to challenge your thought process. I cannot change your mind or beliefs for you. It must be done of your own volition, which means you make a choice! Just know that the Holy Spirit is willing and ready to help you through this!

How to Transform Broken Beliefs:

1. **Face it:** What is the lie you are hearing or telling yourself?

2. **Trace it:** Where did the lie originate from? Broken beliefs are a result of real-life experiences or trauma that occurred. For example, if your husband or wife divorces you against your will, you may be left with the belief that you are not good enough or unworthy of being loved again. Ask the Holy Spirit to reveal the root of the lie (where it originated from).

3. **Erase it:** Renounce the lie, break agreement with it, and apply the blood of Jesus! Ask God by faith to remove every spot, stain, and label the enemy has tried to define you with. Take back legal grounds from the

enemy and close every door by which he has gained unauthorized access to manifest the lies in your life.

4. **Replace it:** Replace those lies with God's truth about you!

This is where you must put in work! Search the scriptures to see and say God's truth about you! Stop speaking death and start speaking life! Negative self-perceptions and thinking patterns have the power to shape your reality. What you believe about yourself you ultimately become. Scripture tells us in Proverbs 23:7 that, "As a man thinketh in his heart, so is he." Please notice that it says as a man "thinks". Yes, every time you speak a lie about yourself out loud, the more you give life to it. It is safe to say that thoughts unspoken do not always die unborn. If you give the lies a home in your heart, you will feel and see what you are believing. The devil is not really the problem. It is easy to blame him, but a shift in perspective will cause you to see that he is only revealing to you what is in your heart. The enemy cannot make you feel a lie; he did not create emotions, nor does he own yours. Satan can only deceive you into believing the lies rooted in your heart. Permit yourself to know the truth, believer bigger, put on Christ, and move forward in victory! You are a winner! Being an overcomer means you have a choice to become better than you have been in the past, to be better than those who have hurt you. Look at yourself during this time and say, "I give myself permission to let of that which has held me bound for so long. I am free from the hurt, pain, guilt, shame, fear, anger, resentment, bitterness, and unforgiveness!" Faith is tested in bitter and broken seasons. Only God can transform the bitterness and brokenness of your heart into something better. Sweeter. Just like He made the bitter waters of Marah sweet for the children of Israel in the book of Exodus (*Exodus 15:23-25*). Denying yourself permission to be better only keeps you bitter, beloved. And no one wishes to drink from bitter waters. You must unbecome all that God never intended for you to be. Letting go of your comfort, the lies and deception you have believed for so long, and even dysfunctional behaviors can be difficult, but it is doable. Persevere through the process by taking it one day at a time. Focus on letting go one old thing or pattern and replace it with something new over time. Work within the limits of your own capacity, at your own pace, and in God's timing. Be consistent too! If you fall short or get off track, start again. Keep going until you develop a healthy routine. Whatever you do, do not give up in the middle of the process. Many times, we give up too soon. We start murmuring, complaining, and losing hope of becoming and beholding what we petition God for. Sadly, this happens when what we desire most is directly ahead of us. The children of Israel are the prime example of this is in Exodus 15:24, "And the people complained against Moses, saying, "What shall we drink?" Yes, the Lord provided for them in the desert wilderness, but they would not have entered their place of Elim, where there were twelve wells of water and seventy palm trees for them to camp by if they would have given up at Marah *(See Exodus 15:27)*. There is much beauty in the promise of restoration when you surrender the old for the new! Welcome the hard moments that come to build you in this season.

Do not be afraid to ask yourself tough questions and answer them honestly. Learn the lessons and harness the power in the place of struggle by allowing it to refine you, and not define you! More importantly, embrace the sweetness of surrender to God.

Questions to Help Identify If You Are in The Middle of Your Metamorphosis:

1. What lies or old habits are you believing about yourself that are keeping you from relinquishing the old version of you for God's best version of you?

2. Who or what in your life should you be letting go of in this season?

3. Do you feel overlooked, forsaken, lonely, or misunderstood?

4. What do you want in life?

Complete the following journal prompt:

What elements of your life do you look forward to seeing change, and how would you like them to change?

A PRAYER FOR HER RESILIENCE

Heavenly Father, I know that becoming resilient is the measure for whether fundamental change will happen in me and in my life. Help me to feel and embrace the newness of what you are doing in my mind, body, and soul even when it is tough. Remind me that you are always with me and causing all things to work together for my good! I believe that I can do all things through Christ who strengthens me! Give me the strength to move forward! Open my ears to hear and my eyes to see all the opportunities you place before me to live my life unrestricted. Keep my mind in perfect peace as my thoughts are stayed on you (Isaiah 26:3). I give you praise for these things in Jesus' name, Amen!

MADE TO SOAR

STAGE 4:

BUTTERFLY

You were made to Soar! So, when it is your time to fly, please fly high! But it would be best if you crawled first! I know, that was not something you expected to hear. But it is the truth. The thought of soaring is great. It sounds very promising. But what most do not realize is that the butterfly does not emerge out of its cocoon into the air. It crawls out before it takes flight. The reason for this is that it must first expand and dry out its new wings. This significant piece of information alone teaches us a whole lesson. When a butterfly is transformed inside a cocoon, its wings are engorged with the same fluids used to break down its food in the caterpillar stage. Time for a moment of transparency. It is rather disgusting to think about a caterpillar digesting its body from the inside out. But your transformation will require the same from you! A breakdown of the old must occur so that the new can rise. The struggle to emerge from the cocoon is what forces the fluid out of the butterfly's wings and into its body to be absorbed and processed. If deprived of this transformative process, the butterfly's wings will remain filled with fluid, causing it not to fly. Take a moment to ponder on what this is teaching you about your process. One of the main lessons to be learned from this is: **Wait for your wings to dry before attempting to fly!**

From my viewpoint, the fluid that causes the butterfly's wings to expand is like being filled with the power of the Holy Spirit. Water is symbolic of God's Holy Spirit, and it is by His spirit that you are cleansed, empowered, transformed, made whole, and given a new nature. You must be soaked in the significance of the Holy Spirit and sealed in the substance of His word. It is essential for the anointing to take residence in the innermost parts of your being then an outward manifestation of it will follow. You do not what to have the style or appearance of Godliness on the outside but be broken, busted, and disgusted on the inside. Remember, God works from the inside out! Not the opposite. It is from the deepest parts of who you are that the rivers of living water will flow. Do not allow the pressure from people to perform and put your newness on display to push you into heights your wings are not yet able to sustain. Listen, your emergence has already been determined and written in destiny. So, there is no need to rush God or go back and forth with people about when it is your appointed time to soar!

God's glory in you will be revealed through you in HIStiming! And it will be grand enough for all to see. Allow Abba to glance at you first! You are HIS creation, and He wants to marvel at the miraculous, transformative work He does in you before sending you out to the masses. Soak in His word. Remain swaddled in His love, and rest in His significance. He knows the beginning, middle, and ending of your process. Remember that you are fully known, loved, and accepted by Him more than anything else. It would be best if you are fully persuaded of these truths.

There is power in knowing who you are, whom you belong to, and that you are a new creature in Jesus Christ! This is important; otherwise, your faith will be crushed by the resistance you are met with once God's glory is on display in your life.

Yes, there are people attached to God's purpose after your transformation, but some people will also attach themselves to you because of your progress. Some will try to bring you down, and others may not want you. They will want only what they can get from you once their eyes are open to your value. It is all a part of the process! Even Jesus experienced this sad reality. The same people He was sent to save did not believe He was the Son of God. They did not want His presence but wanted his miracles. Even the signs and wonders He performed were not enough for them to believe or recognize He was God in the flesh. At least not until He died on the cross and rose on the third day with all power in His hands! I hope you understand my point. You will be met with much pressure to perform after your transformation. I certainly have been tested and tempted to do so many times. But there is an appointed time for everything under the sun.

Sure, you may have moments of exposure, but you must absorb the fullness of the work the Lord is doing in you. Think about it. Would you rather be overdeveloped and underexposed or overexposed and underdeveloped? Your maturity and development are crucial to those you are designed to inspire, impact, and influence. Butterflies have one purpose once they are transformed; to reproduce. There is no glory in transforming into a butterfly that cannot fulfill its purpose. Malnourished caterpillars or underdeveloped butterflies can transform but risk the inability of being able to reproduce. Why transform if you are going to continue acting, thinking, and crawling around like a caterpillar? Your pain and process have a purpose attached to them. That purpose is to help others like you become healed and set free! Did you know that caterpillars, specifically moth caterpillars, form their cocoon with silk? This creature has the unique ability to shape its place of struggle with something so precious, beautiful, and beneficial to all of us to this day.

Beautiful butterfly, your pain may not seem beautiful

or feel purposeful to you, but it is silk to someone else! You will experience still feeling like a caterpillar, and there will be times you find yourself in more places of struggle. You might experience breakthroughs mentally, emotionally, and spiritually and still enter a setback. If this is your experience, I will be the first to tell you, it is part of the process. Trust God and believe that He is ordering your steps. He knows the ending, middle, and beginning of your journey and process!

Along my journey, I found myself frustrated hearing people preach about the promised land but failing to properly prepare me for the process. I did not want the process because it hurt! The process is the middle of your journey. It is a transitional point in life when you come face to face with seasons of barrenness and brokenness. You may feel forgotten about and forsaken. It appears like nothing is happening in your life during this time, and you do not feel like you are growing or going to obtain the blessing. I know what it is like to be around the blessing but not in it; to lose patience with the process and experience cycles of weariness. As a result, your faith, motivation, drive, and more can become bruised. But take heart, beloved. This is the time for you to anchor your hope in the Lord and remember that God created you to soar! You were not designed to remain the same or stagnate. The process prunes and prepares you for the promise and the *wait* prepares you for the *weight* of God's glory to be revealed.

There will be divine pit stops positioned for you throughout your process. The purpose of a pit stop is for you to pause and refuel, allow the Holy Spirit to put new armor on you, make necessary repairs and adjustments inside of you, and sometimes move you out of the driver's seat to remind you that God is in control. Do not skip parts of your process! You will reenter cocoon seasons due to a lack of patience or pressure from people to abort your process prematurely. God is not in the business of serving anything half-baked or undone. His timing is never late or too early. He is always on time and there is much beauty in waiting and enduring being perfected in your process.

You will be made mature in the things of God. The essence of who you are develops and your wingspan becomes wide enough to accommodate the reach and influence God will give you. The beauty of Godly character becomes your strength for service, not status. You will reproduce for God's kingdom and for His glory! Not your own. People will eat and be filled by the fruit of your wholeness rather than nibble on pieces of your brokenness. The journey of becoming is not easy or comfortable. Healing has layers of hurt that aren't often talked about. It takes new pain to get rid of old pain. So, you must choose your hurt. The enemy is banking on you to abort your process but I admonish you to never give up! Make the most of your journey by enjoying the ups, downs, twists, and turns that come with the ride. It's okay to laugh, smile, and even cry when it hurts. Remember that the right pressure and painful moments are designed to build you, not break you. Godly character, resilience, and the fruit of the Spirit are being developed in you during this time. Do not take any of the lessons for granted no matter the obstacles you face. Keep moving forward toward your purpose and promise!

Remember that resilience is in your DNA; you were built to be an overcomer! Although the struggle is real, the healed, empowered, and resilient woman on the other side of your transformation is real, too! The best version of you is waiting and rooting for you to win! After all, that is what you were created to do! So, keep flapping those wings until the residue of who you once were is expelled and the newness of who you are is revealed. God's rivers will flow through you because His Spirit of life is within you! Your transformation is not just about you. Someone else's healing, empowerment, and evolvement are attached to your resilience and obedience. Don't be the reason their destiny is delayed. Above all else, beloved, I hope that you will find rest in the finished work of Jesus Christ and know that God has given you permission and authority to be and become all that He designed and you desire. He formed HER from the beginning! So, start being HER! I pray the words penned in this book inspired a shift in you. One that will encourage you not to give up in your process because God will never give up on you. Why? Because He loves you too much to leave you the way you are! Is there another beauty in this world you love too much to leave the way they are? If so, honor her by sharing or sowing this book into her life to help transform her into the healed, empowered, and resilient butterfly God designed her to be. Remember, beloved, I am rooting for you and would love to encourage, inspire, and empower you even more! This book is only one of the resources I have created to guide you along your journey. Connect with me at www.Tacondra.com to discover more ways that I can love on you, teach and help mentor you.

Questions to Help Identify If You Are in This Stage:

1. What feels new about you? What looks new about you?

2. What visible evidence in your life proves you have transformed, even in the subtlest ways?

3. Are you ready to soar into your next level? If so, what does that look like for you?

4. Do you feel the need for more help to boost your confidence at this point?

A PRAYER FOR HER TO SOAR

Father, I thank you and give you praise for giving me the grace to grow through my process of becoming. Help me to wait on you to renew my strength so that I can mount up with wings as an eagle and soar into my place of fulfillment through Jesus Christ! I shall run, and not be weary; I shall walk, and not faint! (Isaiah 40:31). Release your anointing of excellence on me to soar in my emotional, spiritual, physical, and financial freedom! Invade my life with your purpose, power, and plans! My hope is in your promise to prosper me and give me hope for my future. Thank you for providing me with everything I need to rise above every circumstance, challenge, and struggle that comes with each level of newness you take me to! I will forever give you praise, glory, and honor for all things! In Jesus' name, Amen.

ABOUT THE AUTHOR

Tacondra L. Brown is a wife, mother, author, speaker, advisor, mentor known as the Beautiful Butterfly who inspires transformation in you so that even greater works can be done through you. Vocally gifted, very insightful, and extremely compassionate, Tacondra is known for her beautiful spirit, contagious presence, her straightforward, transparent, and simple approach to advising others while merging biblical principles with the practicalities of everyday living. Her story reaches the hearts of all people struggling with fear, rejection, worthlessness, inadequacy, broken beliefs, and feeling stuck in life. In every mentoring session, conference, workshop, seminar, or ministry assignment she is given,

Tacondra inspires you to discover purpose in your pain, persevere through the process of transformation, and arise beautifully into your full potential, purpose, and power! Endowed with the gift of storytelling, Tacondra invites readers on her journey of transformation and becoming a glory carrier for God. Her published books include: *Transformed from Pain to Purpose,* and *Beautifully Transformed: Discovering Beauty in The Beast, A 7-Day Healing & Transformation Devotional, MetamorpHERsis: Becoming the Woman You Desire, and All God Designed You to Be.*

Transform with me at:

www.Tacondra.com

References

Definition of "Meta" *www.merriam-webster.com*. Retrieved 2020.09.10.

www.ingramcontent.com/pod-product-compliance
Lightning Source LLC
Chambersburg PA
CBHW070306100426
42743CB00011B/2370